# You Are Not Alone

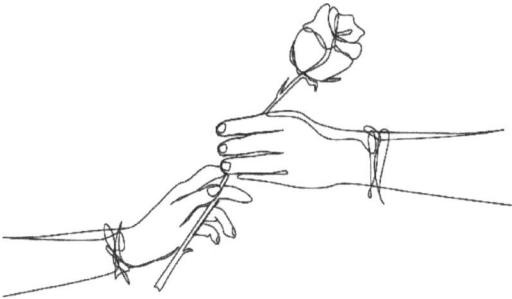

**Also** by Alexandra Vasiliu

**Poetry Books**
*Dare to Let Go*
*Healing Is a Gift*
*Stronger than Anxiety*
*Time to Heal*
*Healing Words*
*Be My Moon*
*Magnetic*
*Blooming*
*Through the Heart's Eyes*

**Children's Books**
*My Love Will Stay Forever*
*You Are a Kindergarten Artist*
*I Love You Day and Night*
*You Can Do Amazing Things*
*You Are a Gift to the World*
*Dear Snowman*
*Have You Seen a Kangaroo?*
*I Am Beautiful and Brave*

**Journals**
*Plant Hope*

# You Are Not Alone

Poems to Embrace Emotional Healing
and Inner Strength

Alexandra Vasiliu

Stairway Books
2025

*You Are Not Alone: Poems to Embrace Emotional Healing and Inner Strength* by Alexandra Vasiliu. Stairway Books, 2025
ISBN-13: 978-1-963003-90-1

First paperback edition, October 2025

Editing services: Melanie Underwood via www.melanieunderwood.co.uk
Cover Illustration: Rusyn via www.shutterstock.com
Book Illustrations via www.shutterstock.com

*For those*
*who fell*
*into the river of pain*

# Contents

## This Is a Sign

If you are going through a trauma,
please allow my heart to tell you
that *you are not alone*.
I know how trauma feels.
I suffered so badly for so long
until I learned
how to walk through places
covered with silent scars.
Now, I am brave enough
to walk this rough path again with you
and lead you out of there.
Let my love show you the way.
This book is meant
to whisper in your heart,
*You are not alone.*
This book is a comforting hug.
Each poem stretches its arms out to you
and embraces you warmly,
*You are not alone.*
Take these soothing words

as a sign of love and strength.
I am with you
in your heartbreak,
in your trauma,
in your loss,
in your grief,
in your fears,
in your sadness,
in your despair.
I am with you.
I will carry the burden of your tears,
and you will hold my poems
in your heart.
Empathy is the lifebelt
that can save us both.
*You are not alone.*

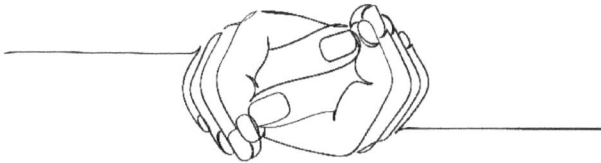

## Your True Date of Birth

You are born on the day
you decide
to heal your emotional suffering.
You are born on the day
you decide
to unapologetically follow
the path of personal transformation.
You are born on the day
you decide
to never look back at your past
through the eyes of fear,
guilt,
and shame.
You are born on the day
you decide
to live fully
and give the best of yourself
to the world.
You are born on the day
you decide

to change yourself for the better
and grow with courage
and determination.
You are born on the day
you decide
to let empathy nourish your heart.
You are born on the day
you decide
to let wisdom infuse your mind.
You are born on the day
you realize
how much love and kindness
you can offer to the world.
You are born on the day
you honor your becoming.
You are born on the day
you start living intentionally
and authentically.

## There Is Hope

It might be impossible to imagine,
but here is a grain of truth:
*There is hope beyond suffering,*
*there is light beyond trauma.*
Standing still
with your heart torn apart,
in the middle of a storm,
is bravery on its own.
Please trust my words.
I am here with you.
I will hold your hand
until the storm passes—
*You are strong and brave.*

## Anyway

Never ask anyone,
"How do you spell hurt?"
Life will teach you anyway.

## Someone You Deeply Care About

If your emotional wounds trace back
to your childhood,
it is time to let that go.
What can you do from now on?
Just do one thing—
take liberating steps.
Move away from self-blame
and start self-reparenting.
Nourish your inner child
with all the love
that was not given to you.
Rewrite your story with determination
and compassion,
and make sure not to pass down your hurt
to the next generation.
While you heal your precious inner child,
your heart will grow stronger.
*You will no longer feel so lonely.*

You will have the gentle power
to hold your inner child
in a warm and permanent embrace.
Hug your wounded child
with all the love
that was not given to you.

Every day,
find the strength
to assure your inner self
that they are safe and loved now.
And while you continue to heal,
let your inner child hear
this loving truth,
*'You are not alone*, little one.
You have me now.'

## Believe in Yourself

Never place your self-esteem
in someone else's hands—
you make room
for emotional abuse,
manipulation,
and trauma.

Believe in
who you are
and in the beautiful person
you can become.
Believe in
your unique potential,
and have faith
in the ability
to chase your dreams.
Treat yourself
with respect,
courage,
kindness,
and honesty.
That is proof of your inner force.

## You Are More Important

If you come from
a very dark place of suffering,
please acknowledge
that you are more than your past.
You are more than your trauma.
You are more than your hurt.
You are more than your tears.
You are more than your nightmares.
You are more than your anxieties.
You are more than your insecurities.
You are more than your failures.
You are more than your inner darkness.
You are more than your sadness.
You are more than your anger.
Don't play the victim card so fast.
Ask yourself,
"Who am I, really?"
Please allow me to tell you this—
you are a pearl
in an ocean of darkness.

You are more valuable than you think.
You are more precious than you realize.
You are more beautiful than you see.
You are more important
than you imagine.
Get up
and wrestle
with the darkness inside.
You can tame the beasts within.
You are much stronger than you think.

## Not to Be Alone

My friend,
healing your broken heart shouldn't be
a solitary process.
As you heal,
you need to water your heart
with love,
understanding,
and wisdom.
Intentionally,
seek out
noble friends
who can support
you emotionally
and treat you
with love
and dignity.
Healing is a process of connection.
*Choose not to be alone.*

## The Unseen Abyss of Trauma

Life has nasty surprises
for each of us.
When life throws them at you,
you will fall into a weird abyss
that sucks you deeper
and deeper.
When you reach the bottom
of this void of
darkness,
someone will tell you,
"You have been going through a *trauma*."
You feel dead inside.
"Where is the exit from this chaos?"
you ask yourself.
Trauma comes
with no pictograms
that can direct you toward
the nearest and safest place.
Trauma has no exit doors.
You are at the bottom

of a horrible pit—
the abyss of suffering.
Don't fill up this depth
with tears—
you will drown yourself
in more sadness.
Don't fill it up
with anger—
you will cement yourself
in an inner jail.
"Then, how can I escape?"
you ask yourself.
There is only one way,
and it is the hardest.
You have to heal yourself.
Healing from trauma means
that you have to climb up
the suffering abyss walls
with your bare hands.
Healing from trauma means
that you must harness
your determination
and inner strength
to enjoy freedom again.
There is no smooth trail.
You will face different challenges
until you get to the top of the crevasse

and overcome trauma.
Stay consistent with your ascent.
Each step you take
is a step of courage
and understanding.
Each breath you take
is a sign of tenacity
and resilience.
Keep climbing,
and think of the only outcome
of your efforts—
the unbeatable view from the top.
You will contemplate
the landscape of freedom.
You will be a conqueror.
*You are meant to live joyfully.*

## Never Truly Alone

In moments of loneliness,
turn inward
and acknowledge
the gentle and wise voice
of your own heart.
Can you hear it?
That soft voice is like a delicate angel
that tries to encourage you
to act with intention
and compassion.
That gentle voice teaches you
great things—
be kind,
help others,
do good deeds,
never harm anyone,
live with integrity
and purpose.
Trust that positive voice,
and let it remind you

that wherever you go,
whatever you do,
you are always accompanied.
*You are never truly alone.*
In moments of loneliness,
listen to the voice
of your good angel
and realize
that *you are never truly alone.*

## No Mask

There will be times
when you realize
you can't cope with trauma.
There will be times
when you notice
that your life turns into chaos.
What will you do?
Will you choose to hide yourself
from suffering?
Will you select a shield
to hide yourself from suffering?
Will you choose
extra hours of work,
more sports activities,
daily shopping,
or over-perfection in your projects?
My friend,
don't hide yourself behind any shield.
The pain will still be there.
My friend,

no shield can silence the screams
of your heart's wounds.
No shield can stop the river of pain
flowing into your heart.
Stop fooling yourself.
Stop playing immature games.
Embrace emotional healing.
Channel your energy into
personal transformation
and emotional development.
Throw away all mental shields.
Jump into the river of pain
and confront your suffering.
Look your pain in the eye,
and embrace yourself
with compassion.
Be the first
to validate your feelings,
"Dear Heart,
you have been through hell."
Be the first
to make a promise to yourself,
"Dear Heart,
count on me.
You are not alone.
From now on,
I will stand by you.

I will never hide
behind ridiculous shields.
I will hug you
whenever you need me.
I will tell you kind words
whenever you need.
We will swim together
through the river of pain.
We will wear
the safest life jackets possible—
courage and strength.
We will navigate the turbulent waters
of suffering
with courage
and perseverance.
We will face
the waves of hardships
with resilience
and inner strength.
Courage and strength
will define us.
One cathartic morning,
we will see the world
bigger and larger than our past.
Dear Heart,
*you are not alone.*
I am here for you."

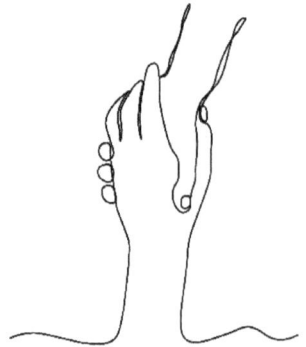

## Once You Understand

Every loss is brutal.
Every loss breaks your heart.
Every loss grinds your face
into the ground.
Every loss humbles you.
How can you cope with it?
How can you accept the new reality?
Don't go through this alone.
Seek support.
Find friends.

Talk to God.
Healing from loss is difficult,
but with every new step,
you will notice
that you change.
You'll become much kinder than ever—
kinder to others and yourself as well.
You will become gentle
with your family and friends.
You will become gentle with everybody.
You will always have a healing word
on your lips
for those around you.
You will show compassion to everybody.
You will change radically.
As your heart softens,
you will be able to integrate your loss
in your story
with love
and meekness.
As your heart heals,
you will become stronger.
You will be able
to show support to other people in need,
reassuring them,
*you are not alone.*

## Trauma Is Not a Noun

Trauma is not just a noun—
it doesn't define anything.
How can the word *trauma* describe
the amount of suffering
and hopelessness
that a person can experience?
Trauma is not just a noun.
It is a knife
that goes deeper and deeper
into your heart,
crushing your universe,
casting you out of the present time
and showing you
that life is more ephemeral than a dream.
Trauma is an exclamation of despair
that instantly kills your reality.

## Finding the Inner Strength

Healing from trauma takes time.
Be patient with yourself.
You don't know how long
it will take.
Maybe a week,
a month,
a year,
or a decade.
It doesn't matter.
Look within,
and start doing the inner work.
Gather the courage
to open the doors of your heart.
Find the strength
to touch your wounds
with the hands
of empathy.
Don't be discouraged.
No matter how hard the inner work is,
please know

that your heart is still beautiful
and precious.

Pour love into your wounds,
tell beautiful things
to your delicate self,
pray more,
and one day
you will admit,
"Trauma couldn't bury me."

## Be Generous Every Day

Do you ever struggle
with low self-esteem?
My friend,
*you are not alone—*
many people feel
that they are not good enough.
But you can overcome poor self-esteem.
Take a few intentional steps
to change your thinking.
Stop being mean to yourself.
Stop believing all the anxiety's lies.
Replace negative self-talk
with positive affirmations.
Treat yourself like a friend.
Be kind to yourself.
Be understanding.
Heal your mind
like you would care for your best friend.
Practice small mental shifts
that will help you

improve self-confidence.
You can start by
focusing on what you can do
for other people.
You can start by
showing empathy to others.
You can start by
being generous every day.
If you don't have anything to give away,
give a smile to your neighbor,
say a nice thing to a friend,
or compliment someone you know.
There is always something good
in your heart
that you can offer to others.
Their joy will boost your self-esteem,
and you will see yourself
capable of incredible things.
That is just a start.
Keep doing good and beautiful things.
Contribute to humanity's healing.
Bring your inner light to life,
and you will notice
that low self-esteem will fade
into memory.
You will make a difference.

## You Feel Disconnected

When you go through a trauma,
you feel like
you are looking at life
through a store window.
You feel lonely.
You feel disconnected.
You are on the other side of life.
You can't stretch your hand
to touch the reality of things.
But at the same time,
you can't continue looking at life
through a store window.
You are not a beggar.
*You are a fighter*.
At that moment,
you will understand an important thing.
You can move forward with your life
only if you break that invisible wall
that separates you from your future.
Where can you find

that kind of force?
It is right within you.
It is right in your heart.
It is the desire for healing yourself.
Take intentional steps
to mend your wounds
and discover your inner strength.
Build resilience.
Healing from trauma is not
a sudden event
like a punch in the adversary's face.
You need time
to defeat that adversary—
your trauma.
Be patient with yourself.
Cultivate self-confidence
by acting with courage
and determination.
Step by step,
you will heal
and be able
to embrace your inner strength.
Remember,
you are a fighter,
and *fighters are never alone*.

## Breaking a Toxic Generational Cycle

If you want to break
a toxic generational cycle,
start healing your thoughts
with this undeniable truth,
'My past is dead.'
Let go of guilt and shame.
Set boundaries unapologetically
in your heart
and mind.
Those boundaries will help you
accept everything that happened
as a finished chapter of your life.
Build a barrier
between now and then.
Break the bad habits
of crossing that barrier daily.
Destroy the obsessive rumination
about your past.
Repeat every day,
"My past is dead."

Don't cling to painful memories
as the only real things you experienced.
Stop now.
Your past is dead,
yet you are alive and strong.
You are not a victim.
Don't choose the underdog role
for your life.
You are a beautiful, brave soul.
You are now here—
strong,
bright,
inspiring,
ready to move on,
ready to create the life of your dreams,
ready to make good choices,
ready to believe in your future.
Be present in your daily life.
Be present in your heart.
Become self-aware
of every moment
of your precious life.
Live intentionally.
Your past is dead.

## Your Suffering Has a Meaning

We all taste pain,
loss,
and disappointment.
We are all part of this human club,
and you are no different.
Your suffering matters.
Your suffering has a meaning.
You will find its purpose
sometime,
sooner or later.
Until then,
find peace in this profound truth,
*you are not alone,*
*you are not weak,*
*you are not lost.*
We are all part of this human club.

## Healing from a Toxic Love

Have you ever felt tired
of not being enough for someone?
I have been there too.
*You are not alone.*
I recall the fear,
the anger,
the despair,
the rejection,
the chaotic feeling of being abandoned,
and everything in between.
This is why I feel for you.
My friend,
you are not alone.
I am here with you.
I am here to help you get over
this traumatic experience.
Set firm boundaries,
and remove all reminders
that keep the past alive.

Let go of co-dependency
and idealized thoughts.
Stop creating endless drama
and romanticizing a toxic story.
Say goodbye to your past
and leave this draining relationship.
These actions will prevent you
from emotional manipulation
and self-sabotage.
You need to heal your mind.
You need to heal your heart.
You need to heal your life.
Reclaim self-respect
and focus intensively and intentionally
on your inner change.
Remind yourself
how brave you have been so far—
you made a wise choice
to move forward.
Continue to be courageous—
you will channel your inner strength into
creating a beautiful beginning.
My friend,
you deserve the light
of a new horizon.

## Hold On

Sometimes,
you may feel lost in this sick world.
Don't allow self-pity
to make room in your heart, though.
Turn disorientation into bravery.
Turn loneliness into bravery.
*You are not alone—*
somewhere,
in this broken world,
someone also feels like you do.
Hold on to hope.
One day,
you will enjoy a healthy friendship.
You will find people who align
with your values and noble dreams.
Until then,
focus on personal transformation,
and persist in creating an inspiring life
guided by your brave and kind heart.

## The Journey Toward Meaning

In every profound journey,
there are three elements:
you,
your trauma,
and your growth.
You can't separate them.
They are interconnected.
They all lead
toward the same destination—
a life of significance.
My friend,
no matter your circumstance,
rise like a phoenix
and create your rebirth—
a life of meaning
and hope.
Never stop.
Never give up.
*You are not alone*.
I am here to support you

while chasing my own dreams
and building my life
with intention,
meaning,
and purpose.
My friend,
let our individual journeys become
a force
of inspiration.
Never stop.
Never give up.
We are not alone.
*You are not alone.*

## You Didn't Deserve That

When someone breaks your heart
and you feel fractured
like a bird
with no wings,
please wipe off your tears.
Find this message
deep down in your heart:
"You didn't deserve that.
You are not your heartbreak.
You are not your pain.
You are not your wounds.
You are not your trauma.
You are not your fears.
You are not your negative thoughts.
Your worth is beyond
your traumatic experiences.
You are beautiful and precious."
Please take the time
to discover all the pearls
that are hidden

deep down in your heart.
Make time for your valuable self.
Discover your hobbies.
Spend time in nature.
Be creative.
Believe in yourself
and your future.
You are a kind soul
who deserves love
and joy.
Be the first
who shows love
to your beautiful heart.
And allow me to whisper
in your heart,
*You are not alone, friend.*

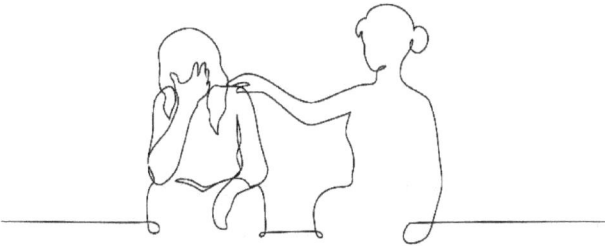

## Overcoming Self-Sabotage

When you sabotage yourself,
you might also struggle
with low self-esteem.
You feel hopeless.
My friend,
there is always a way
to end self-sabotage.
With determination,
embark on a courageous journey
of self-healing.
Start with the easiest things.
Say kind and positive words
to your sensitive self—
'I am worthy of love and grace.
I am worthy of respect and belonging.
I am valuable.
I am strong, brave, and resilient.
I can do beautiful and good things.'
Uproot yourself from negative things.
Detach yourself from people

who abuse you emotionally.
Clear your mind
and set boundaries
to maintain your inner peace—
that is the easiest way
to preserve your sense of clarity
and protect the willingness
to transform your life.
Spread gentleness
in everything you do—
that will be your signature.
One day,
you will realize
you overcame the cycles
of self-sabotage
and low self-esteem.
You will be so thankful
for everything you did.
On that day,
life will smile back at you.

## Simple Reminders

No matter what you have been through,
please keep these gentle reminders
in your heart.
My friend,
*you are not alone*
in a world
filled with so many wonders
and so much grace.
*You are not alone*
in a life that has been given to you
as the most precious gift.
No matter how dark your present is,
strive to grow
into the fullness
of who you were meant to be.
You are an extraordinary ray of light,
and your purpose should be nothing less
than spreading your unique radiance.

## You Are One of the Few People

Society teaches us to avoid pain
and run away from suffering.
The truth is far different.
No one can ever escape suffering.
No one can be exempt from
experiencing pain,
loss,
or grief.
Each of us will go through suffering.
Each of us, including you, my friend.
Rather than imagining an escape,
you should better confront your suffering.
Find its roots,
and heal your trauma.
Grow with strength,
and live your life wisely.
*You are not alone.*
You are part of a particular club
of heroic people
who choose bravery over victimization,

and strength over lament.
You are one of those anonymous warriors
who choose to live with courage,
self-awareness,
honesty,
and determination.
You are one of the few people
who choose to grow out of
all shallow distractions.
You are one of the few people
who choose to stand out with wisdom
and authenticity.
You are one of the few.
You are brave, my friend,
and this is why you are not alone.
You are part of a particular club—
*The Everyday Heroes Club.*

## You Are a Gift

If you don't know your worth,
start a journey of self-discovery.
Spend every day
getting to know yourself.
Treat your precious self
with patience
and kindness.
One day,
you will see
that your heart is a river of love—
great and deep,
clear and beautiful,
authentic and pure.
On that day,
you will realize
that you are not a shadow of suffering
in this world,
but a gift of love and joy.

## Don't Give Up

In heartache,
you discover your inner strength.
In despair,
you fight to rise again.
In the deep darkness,
you yearn for light.
Have you ever thought
how strong you are?
Don't give up on your inner work.
You have so much courage
to look inward
and choose personal growth over despair.
*You are not alone in this journey.*
Many free spirits prioritize self-discovery
and embrace self-worth.
Be one of them,
honoring your authentic and precious self.

## A Lifetime Operation

Do you think
that healing your trauma
is ever complete?
Do you believe
that healing is ever entirely done?
No, of course not,
but being on your healing path daily
is already healing.
And rewarding.

## Your Answer to Challenges

The struggle
with the question 'Why me?'
is a common part
of the human experience.
*You are not alone* in feeling this way.
My friend,
reframe this annoying question.
Heal your mindset—
from 'Why me?' to
'What should I learn from this?'
Embrace personal evolution—
turn 'Why me?' into
'What can I do from now on?'
Nurture yourself with strength—
strength will bring you clarity.
Stop waiting for a sign,
and do something meaningful
with your everyday life—
that will be your answer
to thorny questions.

## You Will Need One Thing

To overcome self-sabotage,
you need one thing—
change your relationship
with negative thoughts.
Acknowledge the presence
of unwanted thoughts,
but instead of talking with them
and confronting them,
focus on nurturing yourself with light
and courage.
Turn your negative self-talk
into positive and realistic statements.
Practice gratitude every day.
Offer help and show kindness to others.
Chase your dreams.
Pursue your aspirations.
Slowly,
you will turn self-sabotage into
self-actualization.

## Emerge from Suffering

If you are heartbroken,
still, go inward.
Grab the shattered pieces
of your heart
and mingle them
with empathy
and forgiveness.
Don't allow a breakup to destroy you.
Look at your heart—
a mosaic of desires and hopes,
still calling for love.
Strive to emerge from suffering
like a phoenix from the ashes.
Turn your trauma into healing.
*You are not alone* in this work—
a resilient community
of fighters
quietly honors your courage
to heal and move on.

## Change Your Perspective

Understand your trauma
as a strict teacher.
Your trauma will teach you
to set emotional boundaries.
Your trauma will teach you
how to rebuild your heart
with wisdom and compassion.
Your trauma will teach you
how to emerge
from the darkness of suffering
as a ray of kindness.
Your trauma will teach you
how to shine again.
My friend,
*you are not alone*;
you are not a victim.
Stop sabotaging yourself.
Just learn your lessons
and strive to grow.

## Everything Is Transformative

People say
that love is a transformative experience,
but so is emotional suffering.
I guess
that life itself is a process of change.
It transforms you
from being emotionally immature
to a rock of strength
and bravery.

## We Are Never Truly Alone

If you struggle with negative thoughts,
please know
that *you are not alone*.
We all endure this internal warfare.
We all deal with mental spam.
*You are not alone.*
Eventually,
many of us bccomc aware of
a different force
in the theater of our minds.
That force is a trusted ally
that helps us
overcome persistent negative thoughts.
That force is our conscience—
the good angel on our shoulder.
We are never alone.
*You are not alone.*
My friend,
let your clear conscience show you
the power of choice.

Let the angel on your shoulder whisper
in your ear
that the choice is always yours.

You can let dark thoughts take hold,
or you can forge a new path
by cultivating kind
and positive thoughts.
Choose to heal your thoughts
and rise from the ashes.
My friend,
choose to turn negativity

into inner strength.
Choose to grow
with light
and accomplish beautiful things.
Choose to begin a new chapter,
and move on
with clarity,
hope,
and purpose.

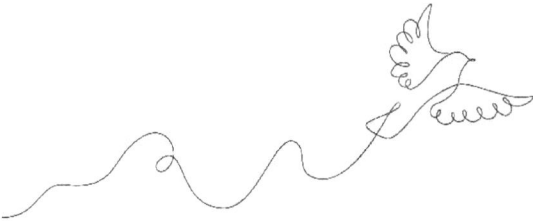

## You Are the Only One

You can't get a vaccine against
emotional suffering.
You can't have surgery
for a breakup.
Is there a surgeon
who could put together
all the broken pieces of your heart?
No, there is no one.
That is the sad truth.
But you are the only one
who can collect the shattered pieces
of your heart
and put them back together
if you decide to face your suffering
and heal your beautiful self.
You are the doctor of your own healing.
You are the only one
who can bring to life what was destroyed.
That is your secret inner strength.

## Don't Keep Looking Back

When memories of the past resurface,
give yourself permission to cry.
But don't spend your life looking back.
Don't stumble over your past.
Focus on the path that is ahead—
your path of healing
and personal transformation.
Offer comfort
to your inner child,
and keep moving forward,
even if you take baby steps.
The more you commit
to your own healing,
the more you protect your inner strength.

## Don't Be Afraid

To heal your inner child,
you must courageously face your past.
Don't be afraid.
Be resilient,
and read your life story
with peacefulness
and emotional maturity.
Then, turn the page
and embrace healing.
That is the only way
to free your inner child
from the past.
Healing is the quiet strength
that helps you move on.

## It Is Just an Intersection

Trauma is just an intersection
in your life.
It doesn't define you.
It is just a point
on your emotional map.
It shows where you come from,
but never where you go from there.
You have the power
to choose your next destination.
I hope
you choose a safe destination.
I hope
you choose to heal.
I hope
you choose to pass through
that intersection.
I hope
you choose to move beyond.
I hope
you choose to find the way forward

to a brighter future.
My friend,
through healing,
you will gain inner strength
to open yourself to life again.
You will be full of
enthusiasm
and hope
for what's to come.
My friend,
I hope
you choose to keep these words
in your heart,
as a helpful reminder.

## Keep Climbing

Emotional healing is a mountain
that you must climb
to reach freedom
and serenity.

*You Are Not Alone*

Some days,
the difficult ascent can feel intimidating—
the mountain's shadow looms larger.
Some days,
you want to give up—
alpinism is a solitary activity.
My friend,
despite challenges,
your healing is non-negotiable.
You have to climb this mountain
so you can heal emotionally.
Don't be afraid.
*You are not alone—*
angels of perseverance
will surround your heart
and climb with you.
Don't overthink.
Courage will be the air
you breathe.
Determination will be the ground
you tread.
Just start climbing this mountain.
You owe it to yourself.
One day,
you will look back
and realize
that the fear

you once felt
was just strength
in disguise.
You will understand
*you have never been alone.*
My friend,
continue your emotional healing.
Never stop your ascent—
this is the way
to discover your inner strength
and unique worth.

## You Have One Priority

Have you ever wished
you could become your ideal self?
Have you ever wanted to be the person
you were meant to be?
If so,
please know
that the priority is not your career.
Above all,
you must do only one thing.
Embrace consistent and gentle healing—
that is the only way
you can gradually become
the best version of yourself.
By actively pursuing your aspirations,
chasing your beautiful dreams,
and fulfilling your potential,
*you will no longer feel alone.*
Your becoming will fill the void.

## Let Empathy Be Your Power

If you want
to heal your emotional wounds,
make more room for empathy
in your heart.
Be kind to your inner child.
Be empathetic
with anyone who is suffering.
Spread kindness
in your heart,
in your mind,
in your life,
and among all the people you meet.
Be gentle all the time.
Life is tough enough for everyone.

## Capable of More Than You Know

Why do you focus so much on
your emotional suffering?
The most beautiful parts of your heart
are still waiting to be awakened.
Activate them
by doing something good
and meaningful
with your life.
Be creative.
Learn a new language.
Learn a new skill.
Offer your help
without waiting to be asked.
Show your kindness.
Be compassionate.
Radiate the goodness
you hold within.
With each passing day,
you will turn sadness into growth.

## Search for an Internal Change

To experience real change,
you don't need a new haircut
or a fancy pair of shoes.
Explore the invisible world
that exists in your heart.
So many wonders and truths
about yourself
are waiting to be uncovered.
Get to know yourself.
Discover the essence of
your beautiful heart.
Cultivate the best parts of yourself
and shape your life
with purpose.
Find fulfillment in your actions,
and *leave no room for feeling alone*.
You can make a real and positive change
in your life.

## The Dark Cage

Trauma is a dark cage
where you dwell
for an unknown period of time.
How can you exit?
How can you escape?

You can't afford to spend
the rest of your existence
in that prison.
Be resilient.
There is a way out—
follow the path of healing.
This action will change you forever.
You will no longer be the same person.
You will learn
to swim against the waves
of suffering.
You will learn
to turn insecurities into strength
and desolation into courage.
You will realize
that everything you have
is you
and your life.
Gather the courage
to step beyond the hurt.
You are made of pure light,
and darkness can't defeat you.
My friend,
reclaim your power through healing,
and you will rediscover the pure joy
of living.

## Five Habits

Add these five habits
to your trauma recovery.
Love yourself gently.
Forgive someone every day,
including yourself.
Dare to let go of
what holds you back.
Detach yourself
from toxic people.
Nurture your mind and heart
with hope,
wisdom,
and compassion.
Step by step,
you will fiercely heal yourself,
and find your inner strength.

## What Tears Tell You

Don't be ashamed to cry
from time to time.
Tears can be proof
that you process your trauma
and try to find a way
to forgive yourself.
Tears can be proof
that you want to embrace healing
as the safest way of living.
Don't be ashamed to cry
from time to time.
Tears are good teachers.

## Love Is Never Small

Trauma happens
when someone tries
to make you feel small or irrelevant.
Please remind yourself,
you are magnificent
because you are made
of an extraordinary essence—
love.
And love is never small,
irrelevant,
or insignificant.
Be the first
to tell this truth to yourself.
Be the first to erase the injustice
of your trauma
through love
and healing.
Be the first
who is responsible
for your personal transformation.

Be the first
to boost your self-confidence.
Be the first
who bravely stands by your heart
and makes a promise,
"Together,
we will come out of trauma
more mature
and determined.
Love is never small,
irrelevant,
or insignificant.
And I love you.
Dear Heart,
I love you.
*You are not alone*."

## Open That Window

Healing is a window
that opens toward
new perspectives on life.
Be curious.
Let healing reveal new paths to you.
You will discover more about yourself.
You will reflect on new meanings of life.
You will meet new people
who will open new doors for you.
My friend,
open the window of healing.
Let the fresh air clear your mind
and spirit.
Are you ready to welcome spring?
Are you ready for the promises
that arrive with this renewed season?
Open that mysterious window,
and stay curious.

## Your Heart Will Know

Healing from trauma is not
an easy recovery.
Sometimes,
it is wise to let go
of your convoluted emotions.
Other times,
standing firm in your truth
and releasing what stands in your way
is better.
Each time,
be brave.
Each time,
be honest with yourself.
Your heart will know what to choose.
One day,
you will realize that
the strength you possess
was forged by everything
you overcame and let go.

## Thriving to Bloom

Have you ever struggled
with low self-esteem?
Take a moment to reflect on yourself.
The way you have treated yourself
has created an ongoing trauma.
That needs to stop.
You can't keep destroying yourself.
Have you ever thought
that low self-esteem is
the silent cry from a heart needing
more love and affection?
My friend,
stop being hard on yourself.
Silence your inner critic.
Stop sabotaging yourself.
Stop believing bad things about yourself.
Show more love and affection
to your precious self.
Say kind words
to your delicate heart.

Every day,
discover one new good thing
about yourself.
Start building positive
and meaningful relationships.
You need good friends
who can show you
how valuable you truly are.
One day,
you will say to yourself.
"I am not perfect,
nor are all the flowers in the world,
yet I am striving to grow
with hope
and bloom
with confidence."

## Focus on Your Growth

Trauma is a merciless thief
that steals from your serene heart.
Can this thief go unpunished?
No, no.
And there is no greater punishment
for this thief
than healing your emotional wounds.
My friend,
heal yourself from abuse,
toxic people,
and negative experiences.
Heal your broken, beautiful heart,
and rebuild your life
with perseverance and courage.
The thief's influence will fade
like a fleeting shadow in the night.
You will find the inner strength
to surround yourself with loving people—
*you will not be alone.*

## For Someone in Their Twenties

If someone asks me
*What advice do you have*
*for someone in their twenties?*
I will tell them this:
"Start loving yourself.
Don't harm yourself by imitating others.
Don't waste your heart on people
who don't care about you.
Don't waste your precious, young years
creating dramas out of nothing,
crying over a toxic relationship,
increasing your anxieties and insecurities,
and burying yourself in trauma.
Don't waste your precious, young years
focusing on people who can destroy you.
They are quicksand
that will swallow your precious heart.
Don't get your soul dirty
to please someone.
Stay away from anything

that could become an addiction—
you will end up becoming a vassal.
Do something
that leaves everlasting traces
behind you.
Get a challenging job.
Learn a new language.
Involve yourself in a ministry.
Discover your talents.
Help a needy child.
Have dreams
and set a purpose in life.
Study hard—
there are so many beautiful things
you can learn.
Have a strong ethic
in everything you do.
Be honest with yourself.
Stay humble
and grateful
for everything that you already have
and everything that you already are.
Discover God early in your life.
Do good deeds in His name,
and keep Him in your life
with devotion
and courage.

Discover who you truly are.
Find who you can truly become.
Work on your inner self
and be the best version of yourself.
Choose wisely the person
with whom you will spend your forever.
Open your eyes,
and notice red flags—
love is never blind.
Don't rush—
love is not a temporary sensation.
Learn to wait—
true love arrives
when your heart is prepared.
Wherever you choose
to go,
be a light
in a world of darkness.
Be a flower
in a world of desolation.
Be a song
in a world of cacophony.
You are already magnificent."

## Your Victory

There is no trophy
for honoring an emotional loss.
There is no trophy
for healing your heart's wounds.
There is no trophy
for overcoming your past.
There is no trophy
for finding peace
after a traumatic experience.
But you must win these invisible wars
and accomplish many courageous things.
And you will celebrate your victory—
your own evolution.
You will be thankful for that.

## The Ocean of Compassion

Trauma left an emotional imprint
in your heart and mind
and almost turned your life
into a caricature.
My friend,
the damage should not be permanent.
You can heal from trauma.
And healing will require you
to dive into an ocean of compassion,
acceptance,
and wisdom.
Take heart
and jump into this ocean.
You will be completely different
when you emerge.

## A Different Healing Approach

If you were emotionally traumatized,
you need to realize
that not only your heart suffered.
Your mind was also harmed
by toxic people.
Now,
your heart and mind need
to heal together.
Don't separate them.
Start healing your thoughts—
your mind will thank you.
Start healing your feelings—
your heart will thank you.
Start healing your life—
you will embark on a journey
to wholeness,
hidden from toxic people.
And you will be thankful for that.

## How Far You Have Come

How can you heal?
Picture this in your mind—
open the door of your heart
and face your wounds
with courage.
Walk into your pain.
Embrace healing
as the only way
to find absolute freedom.
One day,
you will notice
how far you have come.
You will realize
that you no longer live
in a toxic mental place,
yet in a beautiful garden
where you can nourish
your beautiful dreams.

## Become an Alchemist

Are you ready to heal
from your heartbreak?
Go down your rabbit hole,
and accept what happened.
Acknowledge that the past is dead,
but the present is in your hands—
you can shape a better future out of it.
My friend,
get over this heartbreak
and become the alchemist
of your life.
Did you know
that you can change your life
by healing your true self?
*You are not alone* on this path.
Your dreams for a better life are
your constant companions.

## Healing Takes Time

Healing from emotional abuse takes time.
It is a complex process
of rebuilding yourself.
Be patient with yourself.
Be resilient.
Redefine progress.
Small wins always matter—
celebrate them.
Find and cultivate friendships

with kind people.
They will motivate
and encourage you.
They will cheer you up
and celebrate your victories.
Keep company
with those whose hearts are
as good
and loving
as your own.
*You will not be alone,*
no matter how long
your healing journey is.

## Break the Cycle of Pain

Have you ever thought
that the suffering you carry
comes from a very dark place?
Look within.
There are many potential causes
of emotional injury—
from being unloved in childhood
to abandonment and rejection,
from breakups to divorce,
from yelling to domestic violence,
from stigma to bullying,
from financial strain to verbal violence,
from mental abuse to lies,
and many others that generate insecurities
in your life.
My friend,
no matter what you have been exposed to,
remember that

you are capable of
breaking the cycle of pain.
You don't have to adjust to chaos.
You can heal your life.
Dare to understand your emotional injury.
Dare to let go of your emotional burdens,
and heal yourself through compassion.
Dare to turn the narratives of hurt
into a story of empathy.

Dare to overcome your past.
Take it slowly.
Every step of your journey,
remember that
you are much more than your history.
You are a ray of light
willing to emerge
from the shadows of your past.

## Let Me Hug You

Don't be hard on yourself.
Sometimes,
a crucial step in healing
from emotional turmoil
is when you allow yourself to cry,
to grieve for what you lost,
to see toxic people without filters
and let them go out of your life.
My friend,
if you want to cry,
let this open book be your friend—
a shoulder to cry on,
a heart
that can hug you
in the middle of the night.
Cry now
if you want.
*You are not alone.*

I am here.
I will listen to your problems.
I will support you.
Lean on me.
*You are not alone*.
My heart is already full of hugs
for you.

## You Found a True Friend

As you heal,
you come to know yourself better.
You start discovering yourself.
Befriend yourself.
In your authentic self,
find the friend
you always wanted.
As you continue to heal,
*you will no longer be alone.*
You gained a surprising friend—
your precious self.

## Stay Committed

Healing your past implies
rebuilding your life.
You are capable of that,
but every day,
stay committed to love,
kindness,
clarity,
evolution,
and personal transformation.
Don't give up
even when the temptations are big.
Embrace patience,
and nurture yourself
with wisdom.
Include positive habits
in your daily routine,
like listening to soothing music,
coloring a stress-relief coloring book,

taking a walk,
or baking something you like.
Slowly,
you will renew your mind.
Slowly,
you will heal your heart.
Slowly,
you will change yourself for the better.
Slowly,
you will shape a new, brighter future—
one brick at a time.
Fill the new chapter in your life
with goodness,
purpose,
and meaning.

## Your Healing Is a Personal Journey

Every healing journey is personal,
and so is yours.
Choose the journey you want—
smooth,
complicated,
simple,
convoluted,
long,
direct,
super long,
or with shortcuts.
No matter how your journey is,
don't quit.
Don't give up.
Don't bypass the challenges of growth.
Keep healing yourself,
and hold on to hope.
Remember that

in the end,
what matters most
is the destination—
your complete personal transformation.

## From a Toxic Childhood

If you come from a toxic childhood,
please know
that it is not your fault.
Don't think of your life
in terms of guilt and self-blame.
Look at your past in a mature way
and see everyone's fundamental role
in your story.
And then,
look at you
how you were back then—
an innocent child,
full of dreams and hopes.
Healing your inner child
and seeing yourself with clarity,
dignity,
and love
are the greatest gifts

you can have
for the kid you were
and for the adult you are now.
Embrace your inner self
with acceptance and love.

Start to unlearn the myriad toxic things
from your past.
Step by step—
one by one,
remove them from your heart.
Let them go from your mind.
Those abusive things can't define you,
for you are much more precious

than any of your scars.
Be persistent with your inner healing,
even though sometimes,
you will take one step forward
and two steps backward.
It is okay.
On those days,
be gentle with yourself,
and don't give up on healing.
You will eventually find the light
at the end of the tunnel.
Keep practicing emotional intelligence.
Focus on personal growth.
Enrich your life
with positive experiences.
Turn your wounded past into a life
rich in meaningful experiences.
And if some scars never fully fade,
let me tell you this—
make them so faint
that you will barely notice them
in your new, beautiful life.

## Write Down Your Thoughts

On your healing journey,
it is important
to make a to-do list for your growth.

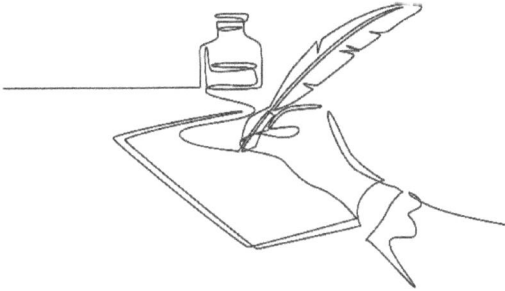

What do you want to change
about yourself?
Write down your thoughts.
What do you want to improve
about your life?
Write down your thoughts.
What kind of relationships
do you want to have
from now on?
Write down your thoughts.
What do you want to achieve
after overcoming your hurt?
Write down your thoughts.
Remember,
despite all your emotional scars
and wounds,
you are precious,
special,
and unique.
You matter,
and you will always matter.

## Turn Tears into Gold

In trauma,
you are not only void,
hurt,
depression,
and tears.
You are the hidden hope
that you can overcome anything
that ruined your life,
and soar again toward love
and freedom.

### You Are Not Alone

Healing is always possible.
Please trust my words
and start working
on your sensitive self.
Every step of the way
and each heavy moment
on your journey,
remind yourself
to be brave
and persistent.
You are wonderfully made,
despite all the traumatic things
you experienced.
You can bring to life
many hidden treasures of your heart.
Heal your sensitive self,
gather all the broken pieces of yourself
and change them into gold.
I know
you are capable
of returning to those scary places
and turn your tears into *gold*—
a new purpose for your life.

## Keep Shining Your Light

In a world full of darkness,
choose to be
a beacon of kindness.
You will be surprised
to discover
*you are not alone.*
In a world full of selfishness,
choose to be
a beacon of generosity.
You will be surprised
to discover
*you are not alone.*
In a world consumed by ego,
choose to spread
the light of love.
You will be surprised
to discover
*you are not alone.*
My friend,
when you realize,

there is a whole community
of amazing people
just like you,
you will cultivate a life
of purpose
and inner beauty.
Embrace this comforting truth now—
*you are not alone.*
In a world full of rays of light,
you are one of them.
You are one
of the many kind people
who choose love,
healing,
and generosity
over inner toxicity.
My friend,
your inner light glows.
I hope
you will be surprised
to discover
how many fabulous things
you can do
with your precious life
from now on.
Many good people will inspire you
to achieve your goals.

*You are not alone.*

You are a radiant light
in a world
that is starved
for authenticity.
Embrace who you are,
and honor your inner beauty.
You are a light.
That is why
*you are not alone*
and *you will never be alone.*

## When You Look Back

One day,
you will clearly see
your beautiful heart.
You will say to yourself,
"Today,
I celebrate my transformation—
I am stronger than I thought."
Trust my words—
one day,
your life will be magnificently different.
You will look back
and see
how far you have come.
On that day,
you will make a promise
to yourself,
"I will keep chasing my dreams—
through them,
I will fulfill my purpose."

On that day,
your story of growth will inspire many.
You will be able
to reassure everyone,
*"You are not alone* on your journey.
*You are not alone* in your struggles."
From that day on,
your heart will become a river
of empathy
and courage.

# Dear Reader,

Thank you for reading my book. I am grateful that, from millions of books, you chose mine to accompany you on your healing journey. I hope my poems keep living in your heart and remind you that *you are no longer alone*. That is the most special gift I can humbly offer to you.

I would love to hear what you think about my book. Please consider leaving a short Amazon review to help spread the word. It only takes a minute and will inspire other readers to discover the healing message of this book. Thank you for your support.

Please remember, *you are not alone*, and you are worthy of love and joy.

Much love,
Alexandra

# About the Author

Alexandra Vasiliu is the author of the bestselling poetry books *Dare to Let Go*, *Healing Is a Gift*, *Stronger than Anxiety*, and *Healing Words*.

Her recent children's books, *My Love Will Stay Forever* and *You Can Do Amazing Things*, have received heartfelt reviews from readers around the world.

Alexandra double majored in French and Contemporary Literature for her undergraduate degree before pursuing her Ph.D. in Medieval Manuscripts.

In her free time, she loves curling up with a book, baking a decadent chocolate cake, or making memories with her family in a US National Park.

Get in touch with her on:

Instagram at @alexandravasiliupoetry

TikTok at @alexandravasiliupoetry

Facebook at @AlexandraVasiliuWriter

Pinterest at @AlVasiliuWriter.

Or, visit her online at <u>alexandravasiliu.net.</u> She loves hearing from her readers.

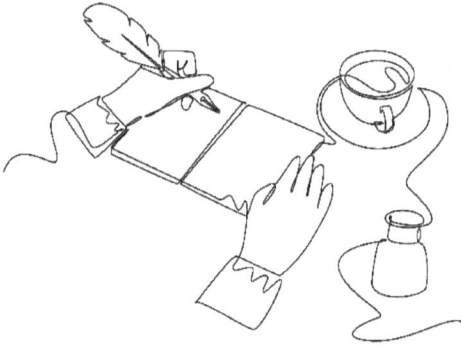

www.ingramcontent.com/pod-product-compliance
Lightning Source LLC
Chambersburg PA
CBHW072005060426
42446CB00042B/1993